Everyday Ways To Enjoy

Success
At Work

ROBB D. THOMPSON

Published in Chicago, Illinois

ISBN 1-889723-75-4
Printed in the United States of America

CONTENTS

EXCEEDING
THE STANDARD

A gainst popular opinion, becoming indispensable in the workplace is easier and more achievable than ever before. In fact, you can become indispensable by cultivating the essential qualities of an excellent employee. Throughout this book, I have listed the most common qualities among those who have achieved great success in business. These attributes are time tested and will work for you if you implement them into your everyday work life. **This list of qualities is not exhaustive by any means, but it lays the foundation for personal achievement in any endeavor.**

I have written this book to provide for you the necessary momentum to press beyond the mediocrity that may be holding back the wonderful future you desire. All of us must fight against the spirit of mediocrity. It attempts to stop us by telling us that we have done enough and don't need to pay such a great price to achieve our dreams.

Every boss, supervisor, and employer is more than willing to promote someone who has rightfully earned it. For many years, promotion has gone to the person who has been there the longest regardless of his production. In fact, he may even be mediocre at best, yet he is the one promoted because there is no one better. What about you? You can change this trend; you can alter the curve by choosing to become an excellent employee.

Don't worry about what other co-workers say or what they think about you. You are not assigned to please them nor do they sign your paycheck. You are employed to be the best employee you can become regardless if others follow or agree. There is nothing wrong with living at a higher standard. In fact, it is necessary if you want to achieve success in the workplace. Sure you may feel pressured to compromise, but the benefits of being the best employee far outweigh the consequences.

Please understand, I am not referring to nor am I encouraging competition in its original meaning. You are not out to defeat the other employees in your workplace. You are on a team and must help others grow.

Don't measure yourself against others. You are competing against yourself, not others. You are not trying to defeat your counterparts or purposely trying to make them look bad. **Always measure yourself against your own standard and strive to surpass that level each and every day.** Stay consistent and you will gain the attention of your employer. Once you gain his attention, you are guaranteed promotion. So allow me to take you through the 20 everyday qualities you must possess to enjoy success at work.

1

LOVE
WHAT YOU DO

"Work Is Love Made Visible."

- Kahlil Gibran

1

There is no substitute for devoting yourself to what you do. There is a longing in all employees to do something they love. Unfortunately, many follow their pocketbook rather than their heart. And although they make good money, they are discontent at their job. Money only brings temporary happiness. It doesn't fill the inner void of purpose. Purpose and passion go hand in hand. If your job's only purpose is to make you rich, then that job will not bring you any lasting fulfillment.

Many have labeled me a "workaholic" or a "type A personality," but I disagree. I don't work. I am devoted to my assignment. I live with passion and express it in everything I do. Sure, there are tasks I don't necessarily enjoy, but the purpose behind the task carries me through. I did not choose what I do for the money; it chose me. In return, I chose it because I am in love with helping people succeed. I am passionate about helping others achieve their destiny.

Do you do what brings you energy? Do you wake up and want to go to work on Monday? Research shows that approximately 95% of employees do not enjoy their job. They stay because of convenience, salary, or fringe benefits. Nevertheless, such motives do not satisfy your longing to fulfill a purpose. The money may bring you a better house, but it won't make a happy home. You may have nice clothes, but your wardrobe won't satisfy you. Although you may move up the corporate ladder, you'll soon find out the ladder leans on the wrong building! Wanting to do what you do is important to your success. Now, I understand that we must go through seasons in life, especially in our earlier years when we don't have the job of our dreams, but we still can move in the direction of what we want to do. **Consequently, you may have to endure seasons of doing things you don't enjoy. Just make sure it is a means to an end, an end in which there's a lifelong purpose, not just an income.**

Ask yourself this question: "If every job paid the same wage, which job would I choose?" Answering this question will free you from money's influence and allow you to discover what it is you truly love to do.

You still may say, "I don't know what I love." That's understandable, so answer these questions to start discovering the right direction.

- *If you could do one thing all day at work, what would it be?*
- *If you could do any job or full-time activity without pay, what would it be?*
- *What type of work or activity gives you the greatest joy and satisfaction?*
- *For what would you like to be known?*

Doing what you love is your choice. No one can make you do anything. If you don't like what you do and you continue simply because of money, begin a pursuit of what you want to do. It will take time, but even a one thousand mile journey starts with the first step.

One final reason men and women do not do what they want is fear—fear of failure—fear of not making enough money—fear of the unfamiliar. The only way to overcome fear is to face it. The giant named FEAR always seems more terrible than he really is. Run toward your giant and face him head on.

Do what you love, and your life will be fulfilled. Go after your dreams. Live with passion and never settle for something you ultimately don't love to do. Can you imagine actually waking up wanting to go to work? I do, and I believe the same can be true for you!

*"Find Something You Love To Do And
You Will Never Have To Work A Day In Your Life."*

-Harvey Mackay

LESSON TO LEARN

Every May, corporations across America receive a deluge of applications from college graduates seeking employment. After the strenuous hiring process, new employees must be trained for their particular assignment. The personnel responsible to train new employees is often frustrated by young men and women who think that having a college degree means they don't need training. Some trainers have resigned to this annual problem as an inevitable challenge within the corporation.

One trainer, Maggie McConnell, found this "problem" to be her golden opportunity. She too went to the company after college with hopes of finding a worthwhile career. She was disillusioned, though, by the tedium and lifelessness of computers, emails, memos, and letters. When the company announced they were looking for someone to train new recruits on the company's general procedures, Maggie volunteered. She immediately adapted to her new responsibility as though she had slipped on a well-fitting glove. Her first conversation with new employees startles and excites them as they catch the genuine love she has for her position.

In the recent years Maggie has served in that capacity, the new employees have generated greater productivity than ever in the history of the company. They often take a moment to thank Maggie for her contagious love for what she does.

PERFORM
AT YOUR BEST

"*Always Live In Pursuit Of Becoming
The Expert In Your Chosen Field
Of Endeavor.*"

- Robb Thompson

2

Life is not worth living if you don't give it your best. What reward do you have if you live half-heartedly? There is no joy in doing an average job. Do every task as if you were to sign your name on the finished product. Ask yourself, "Do I want others to know that I did this?"

Only we know when we do our best. Only we decide when we give the extra effort. It is at the offering of our best that we get noticed by those who can promote us. Doing your best must become a daily habit. Like all habits, this one is formed through repetition. As you do your best in one area of life, you'll discover that it's contagious—it spreads to everything else you do!

I can't imagine doing something and not giving my best effort. I would feel as though I wasted my time and the time of those who counted on me. What if the barber didn't do his best? How about the tailor? The mechanic? The surgeon? You may say, "They're expected to do their best because someone else is affected by their mistakes." What about us? Aren't people affected by what we do? And can you honestly expect to receive what you are unwilling to give?

The coach who doesn't do his best cannot expect his players to give him their best. Nor can a mediocre boss expect excellence from his employees. The boss who doesn't do his best indirectly encourages others to be average.

What You Do, No Matter Who You Are, Affects Those Around You.

Don't expect from others what you are unwilling to give. Wake up with the commitment to do your best no matter how you feel or what you do. When Michelangelo's assistant asked him, "Why are you taking so much time painting the corner of this chapel? No one can see it." Michelangelo responded, "God can see it!" And God also sees your work. He sees the final touch you make and every corner you cut. Every time you approach life with the "just good enough" attitude, you abort your future promotion.

Doing your best is part of the meaning of the word excellence. Excellence is the passionate pursuit of distinction, and distinction requires you to do your best. What makes you different from those around you? I guarantee you this: those who do their best are in the top ten percent of employees in any corporation. Post this question where you can see it often:

IS THIS THE BEST I CAN DO?

Think back to your days in school. How many people do you know who really did their best in class? How many of your classmates went to lectures prepared, excited, and ready to participate? How many read the textbook, asked questions in class, and did more than what the professor assigned? Very few, no doubt!

Since those are the same people in the workforce today, why is it any different? The same people who trudged through school are those who hold the majority of jobs. And just as only a few students in the classroom did their best, only a few people in the workforce give their all to their job. Unfortunate as this is, it means that there's plenty of room at the top for anyone willing to do their best.

"When We Do The Best We Can,
We Never Know What Miracle Is Wrought
In Our Life Or The Life Of Another."

-Helen Keller

LESSON TO LEARN

The owner of a growing fancy chocolate company located in New England has a revolutionary philosophy that he adopted after years of working in a large, cold, chocolate processing plant. At the plant, the employees were discouraged from talking, forbidden to eat any of the chocolate, and expected to keep to their work.

The plant experienced massive turnover rates, and their profit margins steadily declined. The man, now into his more mature years, decided to open up his own chocolate company. The building where the chocolates are made is full of bright colors. The chocolates are handmade, and the employees are encouraged to make mistakes, since they could lead to new ideas.

Once the final product is completed, the employees are asked to put their own chocolate trademark on it to show that it was their handiwork. What the owner has created with this philosophy is a staff of employees who are eager to do their best work, and his profits have reflected their remarkable efforts.

ADOPT A WILLING ATTITUDE

"There Are No Menial Jobs,
Only Menial Attitudes."

\- William John Bennett

3

Have you ever come across an individual who is willing to do whatever you ask regardless of its inconvenience? This is the employee of which every boss dreams. A study in *Psychology Today* stated that bosses would rather have a happy and willing employee over a competent, unwilling employee. A willing person can learn a skill, but very rarely will a talented novice change his attitude.

Attitude is expressed in many ways, but here are three prominent indicators: **countenance, body language,** and **tone of voice**. Your **countenance** is the outward expression of your inner attitude. You show what you feel on your face.

Body language is also an attitude indicator. Any time you do something you really enjoy, your body takes on a different posture. You stand straighter and poised for action. When asked to do something you feel is bothersome, your shoulders drop and your posture sags. Changing your body posture can actually alter your attitude. If you stand up straight, keep your head up, and smile, your attitude will follow.

The last indicator of your attitude is your **tone of voice**. Your verbal reply to instructions reveals whether or not you are willing. Willing individuals have energy in their speech. They communicate with enthusiasm and passion. Infuse your words with passion instead of the monotony and dullness of most people's voices. You can consciously change any of these three aspects and your attitude will follow.

Your Perception Of Life Determines Your Attitude Toward Life.

So from where does a negative attitude come? The main source is wrong perspective. People perceive other people and situations around them through the lens of negativity. But *how do you perceive those around you? How do you perceive your work environment? How do you perceive your boss and your coworkers?* Your perception determines your attitude, good or bad. Change your perception and your attitude will follow suit.

Do you see work as a way to make money or as a way to express your God-given talents? Do you see your boss as a taskmaster using you for his own glory, or do you see him as someone who helps you get to the top? Your perception makes all the difference. There are always two ways to perceive everything, and the choice is always yours to make! Your "attitude determines your altitude." The following poem depicts that principle so well.

ATTITUDE

I woke up early today, excited over all I get to do before the clock strikes midnight.

I have responsibilities to fulfill today. I am important. My job is to choose what kind of day I am going to have.

Today I can complain because the weather is rainy or I can be thankful that the grass is getting watered for free.

Today I can feel sad that I don't have more money or I can be glad that my finances encourage me to plan my purchases wisely and guide me away from waste.

Today I can grumble about my health or I can rejoice that I am alive.

Today I can lament over all that my parents never gave me when I was growing up or I can feel grateful that they allowed me to be born.

Today I can cry because roses have thorns or I can celebrate that thorns have roses.

Today I can mourn my lack of friends or I can excitedly embark upon a quest to discover new relationships.

Today I can whine because I have to go to work or I can shout for joy because I have a job to do.

Today I can complain because I have to go to school or eagerly open my mind and fill it with rich new tidbits of knowledge.

Today I can murmur dejectedly because I have to do housework or I can feel honored because the Lord has provided shelter for my mind, body and soul.

Today stretches ahead of me, waiting to be shaped. And here I am, the sculptor who gets to do the shaping.

What today will be like is up to me. I get to choose what kind of day I will have!

-Author Unknown

The Greatest Weakness Attitude Possesses Is Its Incapacity To Remain Hidden.

BE PLEASING

Pleasing others should be our motive in everything we do. If bringing pleasure is your motive, your attitude will remain positive, even if you aren't recognized or acknowledged. If your motive is personal glory, your attitude will go sour at the slightest inconvenience.

I always encourage my employees to please those above them. No matter how much others may mock you for being a "brown-noser," you will enjoy the benefits that bringing pleasure adds to your life. Any boss favors the person who is pleasing to them.

Employees spend too much time trying to please their coworkers instead of their supervisor. The person whose approval you want is the one who can promote you, not those on the same level as you. Your top priority is to please your boss. Ask yourself what you can do for him and how you can make his life easier. Make the choice to do anything in your means to please him. In the long run, you benefit as well.

The first step to being pleasing is to focus on the details. When you pay attention to the small details, you never fail in the big things. **Neglect of detail is your one-way ticket to demotion.** A boss simply won't put up with a reoccurring oversight of details. Don't make your superior search for help elsewhere.

LESSON TO LEARN

The whole crew of flight attendants was friendly, but Jeanne stood out. She treated Mr. Smith like he was someone special. His initial gruff greeting didn't scare her a bit. She must have seen something in his tired eyes that told her he wanted someone to care about him. She couldn't have thought he had anything to offer her—his wispy hair and flannel shirt gave no hint of affluence. As far as he could tell, there was no reason for her to treat him as warmly as she did.

During the long flight, she became exactly what he needed her to be—genuine, caring, and patient. He stepped off the airplane refreshed, like he was young again. He didn't have the means to thank her for her kindness—his gratitude was all he could offer. Somehow, though, he thought that was all Jeanne was hoping for.

DO MORE
THAN YOU MUST

4

"*Giving People A Little More Than What They Expect Is A Good Way To Get Back More Than You'd Expect.*"

- Robert Half

4

Many refer to doing more than you are paid to do as "going the extra mile." I touched on the importance of doing your best, but this concept goes one step further. Although you may do your best concerning what is required of you, it may not get you promoted. You arrive at promotion when you do more than what is required. Just because the boss didn't ask you to do something does not mean you aren't supposed to do it. Take the initiative and go the extra mile.

Promotion Is Never Granted By Performing The Tasks You Are Already Paid To Do.

Those who only do what is required should not expect any type of promotion. **Promotion only comes to those who do more than they are paid to do.** If you are paid to do a task, and you complete the task, why would you be promoted? You did what you were paid to do. But if you did more than what was asked, that gives you a reason to expect promotion.

A son who is expected to keep his room clean cannot ask for a special treat because he did it. If he is asked to clean his room and he cleans the whole house, he rightfully earns a reward. He did more than was required, and therefore he deserves a prize. What have you been asked to do? Do it with excellence and to completion. Only then are you qualified to go the extra mile.

Once you complete your assignment, go beyond what was asked by doing more than you were paid to do.

Promotion is granted to those who go the extra mile. Take the initiative to reason what the boss would want done, and then get started on it. What employer wouldn't want such an employee? A boss is more than willing to promote this type of individual.

Ask yourself, "Have I done what was asked of me? If so, what can I do to go the extra mile? What would my boss love for me to get done without him having to ask?" Do it immediately and you will reap the reward of promotion!

"You Need No Fear Of Competition
From The Person Who Says,
'I'm Not Paid To Do This And I'll Not Do It.'
He Will Never Be A Dangerous Competitor
For Your Job. But Watch Out For The Fellow
Who Remains At His Work Until It Is Finished
And Performs A Little More Than Is Expected Of
Him, For He May Challenge You At The Post
And Pass You At The Grandstand."

- *Napoleon Hill*

LESSON TO LEARN

Diane created Fine Foods Delivery Company from the expression of a love for cooking and serving she inherited from her mother, but the dream of making a living from it turned into a management nightmare.

Her staff consisted of delivery drivers, customer service representatives, a secretary, stock boys, marketers, and in-house chefs for catering. When business was good, she hardly noticed the corners being cut by almost every employee. As business slowed and competition won many of her customers, she realized something was wrong. Those she had trusted with responsibilities were doing just enough to get by.

Diane held a staff training night (which she catered herself), and she challenged them to improve their performance for the sake of their own character, not just the business. Only a few of the employees responded to her challenge, but what a difference it made! Though she hadn't been able to give them a raise before, their greater efforts during the day and their added hours off the clock revitalized business enough to reward those few.

Within a few months, Diane had replaced seventy-five percent of her staff, and profits reached new records every month. Diane made it worthwhile for the employees that carried her company to success even before they saw a benefit for themselves. They were rewarded because they were willing to go the extra mile.

MANAGE
TIME WELL

*"Time Is The One Things We All Possess.
Our Success Depends Upon The Use
Of Our Time And Its By-product,
The Odd Moment."*

- Arthur Brisbane

5

Life is measured by time. Everyone has twenty-four hours in a day. **How we use those twenty-four hours determines the outcome of our lives.** How well do you manage your time? Do you have purpose in every day? Hour? Minute? Second? You may think that is impossible, but high-performers know where their time goes and why it goes there. They have purpose in every second.

Time is the tool God gave us to create any future we desire. The rich don't receive twenty-five hours while the poor only get twenty-three. Everyone has twenty-four hours. Time is an inexplicable resource given to mankind. With it, all things are possible; without it, we cease to achieve.

A Great Life And A Mediocre Life
Cost The Same Price—Time.

Every tomorrow is created by every TODAY! If you don't like your today, just know that it was created with the time you were given yesterday. If you want a better tomorrow, change the way you use your time today.

If you were to take an inventory of your time for a week, would the results frighten or satisfy you? Be honest. We want to believe that we manage our time well, but the truth is that we can all manage it better. It has been said, "Time is our greatest commodity." I certainly agree. There is no greater possession than time, but the fleeting thing about time is that it has to be used. You cannot carry it over to the next day. You must use it right here and now. If you don't know what to do with it, then surely you will waste it.

You may not like the way your life is turning out, and you may feel that things should be better than they are. Surely, we all have thought this at one point or another, but can we change it? Certainly! Change the use of your time, and you'll change the course of your life.

Although you may have wasted millions and millions of seconds (we all have) that soon add up, you still can change. You can decide today that you will manage your time in such a way that you create a better tomorrow—a future you want. You are the master, and time will create whatever it is you desire.

Time Is The One Thing Over Which We Have Been Given Complete Control. Your Success Depends Upon How You Spend Your Time.

We all have our standard eight hours on the job. History shows us, though, that no self-made millionaire worked from only nine to five. They all used the time after work to their advantage. **Research tells us the difference between the rich and the poor is how they use their time between 6:00 and 9:00 p.m.** One may go home, watch TV, have a meal, and take a nap. Another may stay late at work, read about improving at the job, and spend an hour learning a new skill. Can you guess what will happen to both individuals after two, five, and even ten years? They no longer will be in the same class. How they use their time determines the outcome of their life.

Ask yourself these questions:

1. *What is the most valuable use of my time right now?*
2. *What is my highest priority task?*
3. *What hour of the day can I set aside to work on personal development?*
4. *How will I log where my hours go for the next week?*
5. *Who manages their time well? When will I set up a meeting with them to learn from them?*

All Of Us Have Twenty-four Hours In A Day.
How We Spend Those Twenty-four Hours
Determines The Outcome Of Our Lives.

LESSON TO LEARN

Medical school taught Brittany Richards much more than treating the sick. Her demanding course load forged her ability to make the most of her time. Her part-time job and social obligations tightened her schedule even more. By the time she completed her residency, she thought she had mastered her own clock.

As a physician, she experienced an overload of impatient patients. Her waiting room was often crowded beyond comfort. Despite Dr. Richards' ability to manage her own time effectively, the demand for her attention grew. Her responsibilities at home were no small matter, either. The stress of life forced her to make changes.

Her attention to patients couldn't lessen because it was the cornerstone of her practice. Instead, she delegated every task that could be handled by a nurse or an office aide. All the non-immediate issues were assigned to after office hours. Even at home, she intentionally took time to relax rather than fitting it between phone calls and paperwork. Knowing her need for sleep, she gave herself a non-negotiable bedtime that she followed faithfully.

These changes, among others, were by no means easy, but within a few months they produced a relatively peaceful atmosphere that was healthy, profitable, and enjoyable.

INITIATIVE

TAKE

6

"*They Always Say That Time Changes
Things, But You Actually Have
To Change Them Yourself.*"

- Andy Warhol

6

"*If it is going to be, then it is up to me,*" is a famous saying by motivational speaker, Zig Ziglar. Most successful people I know are people of action. They constantly go, do, and achieve far more than the average person.

Your success lies in your ability to take initiative. As an employee, your promotion is hidden within the seed of your actions. What can you do that will impress your boss? What can you do to become more skilled at what you do? Be creative. Think of new ways something can be done or a new position that is needed. Go to work and make it happen. Take immediate action whenever you get an idea. I wonder how many ideas go to the grave never to be acted upon. Begin now—not tomorrow, not next week, but today—to seize the moment and make this day count. Yesterday is gone and tomorrow may never come.

Remember the story of Rudy, the young man who had a dream to play football for Notre Dame? His dream became a reality only after he took initiative.

Do you want a promotion? I haven't seen any boss hand them out like they were candy. You have to earn them. This happens when you take initiative—put your ideas into action, take on tasks that normally wouldn't be assigned to anyone, and do things before you are asked.

Man Cannot Fail Without His Consent And
He Cannot Succeed Without His Participation.

A BRIEF WORD ON PROBLEM SOLVING

Most people don't understand the correlation between solving problems and rewards. **Your value is linked to your willingness to solve problems for others.**

What problems can you solve for those who are currently further up the ladder of life? What can you do to make their lives better? The problems you solve also determine how you will be remembered. The greater the problems, the more you will be rewarded.

All you have to do is recognize a problem and put some thought into a solution. Be careful, though, to avoid bringing a problem to your boss's attention without a solution on hand. You only aggravate a person who already has enough to balance, and you get no reward when the problem is eventually solved.

The existence of a problem proves there is a solution. You are paid by your employer to solve the problems he gives you, but if you want to be promoted, then solve greater problems. Posture yourself as a "go-to" person.

BENEFITS OF SOLVING PROBLEMS

1. **Solving problems creates favor with your boss.** You will become indispensable, and in order for your boss to benefit more greatly from your service, he must move you to a place of greater responsibility.

2. **Solving problems motivates the rest of the team.** When you solve problems for your employer, your coworkers will respond in one of two ways. They will be inspired to do the same, or they will resent you for making them seem less valuable.

3. **When you solve problems, your self-confidence increases.** Your sense of worth is proportional to how valuable you are to the people around you. Solving problems boosts your confidence. Knowing you have pleased your boss lets you lie down at night, satisfied with your day's work.

One final note: Don't try to solve problems you can't handle. Find those you can, and start by solving them. As you grow in problem solving, what once seemed impossible will become possible. Take your time and be patient. Problems are not always easy to distinguish, but when you see them, be the first one to solve them. That is where your difference lies.

Becoming Indispensable In Life Is Easy;
Solve The Problems Others Refuse To Solve.

LESSON TO LEARN

Nate grew up in a home where both of his parents worked full-time jobs just so they could pay the bills for the family. At sixteen, Nate got his first job. By twenty-one, he had worked at thirteen different jobs, rarely making much more than minimum wage. Frustrated with his own shortcomings and determined to improve his circumstances, he enrolled in night courses to study business.

For the first time in his academic life he was motivated to learn. During the two summers previous to graduation, he interned at a large marketing firm downtown, receiving a meager stipend for his efforts. Shortly before graduation, he was offered a full-time position at the firm, which he graciously accepted. Spending two summers in the office taught him much of the responsibilities of the different departments, the protocols for working with clients, and even a bit of the company culture.

As an employee, he quickly learned the remainder of the workings of the company, but he also noticed the problems the firm faced. When Nate started coming up with solutions for those problems, his employer was surprised, and his coworkers were resentful. Within a few years, Nate's actions and dedication as well as his humble attitude toward the office staff promoted him past many of his seniors and earned him a salary much nobler than his parents had ever known.

RADIATE
ENTHUSIASM

7

"Enthusiasm Is The Fuel That Propels You Into A Successful Future."

- Robb Thompson

7

What is the major difference between the person who perseveres and the person who quits? **ENTHUSIASM!** Think back on your past and see if you can recognize the times you lost your enthusiasm. You more than likely threw in the towel shortly afterward. I'm guilty of this, and I still have to work on being enthusiastic in some of the things I do.

Enthusiasm is the fuel that drives you to excel. Without it, you won't persist in any endeavor. It is possible to lose your enthusiasm. The good news is it can be rekindled—for work, marriage, exercise, and even learning.

> *One Feels The Noblest And Acts The Best*
> *When The Inspiration Of Enthusiasm Drives*
> *Him Onward Toward The Attainment*
> *Of A Well Defined Goal.*

How do you define enthusiasm? Do you see it as a feeling, an emotion, or a mental state? Enthusiasm comes from two Greek words. The first is *Theos*, which means God. The second is *En-Ta*, which means *within you*. The original meaning of the word, then, is God *within you*. Enthusiasm is allowing God to express Himself through you. Allow God's emotions, ideas, and creativity to flow through you into everything you do.

Whatever your occupation may be—banker, baker, coach, minister, printer, officer, superintendent, or teacher—you will encounter many struggles before you will achieve your dreams. But you can overcome with the force of enthusiasm. Ralph Waldo Emerson said, *"Enthusiasm is the mother of effort and without it nothing great will ever be achieved."*

HOW TO DEVELOP ENTHUSIASM

1. **Stay focused on your objective.** Whatever you focus on grows. The more you place your thoughts on your main objective, the more your desire to attain it grows. Put your goals before you every day. Paint a picture of them onto the canvas of your mind. This simple practice refreshes the enthusiasm you once had.

2. **Take action.** Emotions always follow action. As you act the part, you soon feel the part. Act enthusiastically even if you don't feel like it, and you soon will see a transformation in the way you feel.

> *"If You Want To Be Enthusiastic,*
> *Act Enthusiastically."*
>
> -Dale Carnegie

Lesson to Learn

At a large corporate office and warehouse in the Midwest there's an older fellow whose contagious grin brings a holiday-like cheer to passing employees. Gene works as one of the janitors for the packaging department. On his supply-closet-turned-office door are taped newspaper comics of custodial workers.

The only clue that Gene is well into his sixty's is his bright white head of hair and whiskery jaw line. He has the pep of a man in his twenties and the physique of a runner. Dressed in a flannel shirt, blue jeans, and a pair of sneakers and packing an arsenal of spray bottles, Gene's attitude at work radiates an enthusiasm that far surpasses that of even the most promising executive in the office. Gene hasn't made millions of dollars, and there isn't much room for promotion in his line of work. He could choose to be a gruff old man, resentful of the hundreds of young men and women who rush past him every morning on their way to their computers, faxes, and emails.

Instead, there's a pervading gratitude in his eyes and in his smile that celebrates every moment of life. The employees could forgo one of their lunch breaks to learn a thing or two about enthusiasm from Gene, as it is more valuable than a midday meal.

PERSONIFY
DILIGENCE

8

"He Who Labors Diligently Need Never Despair, For All Things Are Accomplished Through Diligence And Labor."

- Menandor of Athens

8

Diligence is the speedy attention to an assigned task. Diligence is getting the job done promptly and in excellence. Do you act quickly when your supervisor asks for something? Do you do it immediately or wait until later? This is yet one more difference between those who are mediocre and those who excel. Your immediate attention to an assigned task proves to your boss that he is your priority. He sees you take notice of what is important to him.

Are you known as a completer or as one who leaves projects unfinished? Practice finishing tasks more strongly than how you began. Complete everything you start unless you know it has become unnecessary. Make sure to finish every project you start. Otherwise you will have the memory of incompletion every time you think about that project. When assigned a task, don't stop until you are finished.

One effective technique I use is to work on my most important task until completion. It means not starting another task before the one at hand, the most important one, is completed. Diligence is the key to completion. Be known as the person who always completes the assigned task.

An Excellent Employee Gives Results— He Doesn't Give Regrets.

Become results orientated in everything you do. Your boss is focused on results and production, not on your sincere intentions. **When asked to do something, immediately get to work until it is completed.** If you do a little here and a little there, you double or triple the amount of time it takes. Instead, work on it until you can say, "It is finished."

Practice this, and you will develop the quality of diligence in your life. It carries over into others areas, too, creating rapid change. Ask yourself these questions:

- *To what areas can I apply diligence?*
- *Are there any projects I have not completed?*
- *Do I finish stronger than I start?*
- *Am I known as the one who gives immediate attention to an assigned task?*

"Diligence Is The Mother Of Good Fortune."

-Miguel De Cervantes

LESSON TO LEARN

Many years ago, I worked for a well-known parcel delivery service. That job was essential to my development; it helped me get off the ground financially and it gave me a few lessons in character. I would regularly approach my boss in the morning and say to him, "Sir, I am here today to help you get a promotion. Whatever you want from me is what I'm going to give and even more." Now, my boss was not a particularly kind man, and he didn't care for my personality. He never showed any sign of graciousness toward me, and he regularly chimed in with the fellow drivers to belittle me. Still, none of that mattered to me. I meant what I said. I wasn't looking to be a friend of the boss. I desired to do my job the best way I knew how.

There were trying moments to say the least, but all the ridicule I endured was worth it. I was often given two or three times as many packages to deliver than the other employees, yet I always seemed to finish before them. They'd say, "Hey Thompson, what are you doing? You're making us look bad!" The truth is, they made themselves look bad. They lived at the lowest acceptable standard. I lived at the highest. What was the result? Well, here I am today, getting to do what I love—helping people all around the world.

EXEMPLIFY
SELF-DISCIPLINE

9

*"An Excellent Employee Doesn't Require
Oversight And Always Welcomes Inspection."*

- Robb Thompson

Self-discipline is the ability to do what you know you need to do when you need to do it, whether or not you feel like it. The single most important quality for success is self-discipline. Self-discipline takes you to places and keeps you there while your enthusiasm builds. Your job requires of you to do things you won't necessarily feel like doing. This is where you must apply self-discipline and complete the task, regardless of how you feel.

It is not what you intend to do or what you know to do that determines your future. It is whether or not you discipline yourself to pay the price, over and over, until you finally obtain your objective.

Those who are trusted to manage themselves and their time are given more responsibility. Discipline allows you to master your time, emotions, and desires. The urge to procrastinate is suppressed by the disciplined person. You need self-discipline to delay gratification, to organize your work area, and to work on your highest priority task.

There are days when you don't feel like going into work. There are times when you don't feel like completing a project. You must apply self-discipline and decide to do what needs to be done, regardless of how you feel. Practice this, and it becomes more natural. The purpose of discipline is solely to create a habit. **We are a living expression of the habits we develop, positive or negative.** Discipline yourself to do what you are assigned to do. This practice alone will advance you beyond your contemporaries.

> *"Simply, Self-discipline Enables You*
> *To Think First And Act Afterward."*

> *-Napoleon Hill*

LESSON TO LEARN

One employer said to his aspiring novelist, "Progress is a matter of self-discipline." The employee didn't understand. "C'mon," he said, "self-discipline is important for athletes and soldiers, but all writers need is a good idea." The boss smiled at the aspiring writer's oversight. "How many times when you were trying to come up with a story did you check your email? How long were you on the phone? How many times did you wander away from your desk to get a snack? Is it any wonder you haven't come up with a good storyline?" The writer saw what his boss meant.

To get the job, he spent weeks writing and perfecting his application short-stories, hardly leaving his chair but to satisfy his hunger or go to the restroom. He produced a number of highly acclaimed stories in his first months on the job, but after that he seemed to forget the effort it took to take him there. His boss had been gracious enough to correct him gently. Nonetheless, the writer knew he'd better adjust his habits, or he would be released to waste his own time.

What followed was remarkable. He didn't produce any masterpieces for a number of years, but he did notice every irrelevant thing that fought for his attention. By refusing to give in to his every whim, he refined his character so much so that in the following years he was able to write nationally recognized stories which brought substantial income to himself and his employer. Discipline was his ticket to promotion, and by it he became famous for his work.

10

PRACTICE
ASSERTIVENESS

*"The Basic Difference Between Being Assertive
And Being Aggressive Is How Our Words And
Behavior Affect The Rights And
Well Being Of Others."*

- Sharon Bower

10

Being assertive is the balance between being aggressive and being passive. Aggressive employees seem demanding and controlling. Passive employees are afraid to express their feelings, voice their opinion, and share new ideas. Coworkers dread working with the aggressive type. Working with the passive is no better, though, because they add no value to the effort. Consequently, both personalities are ineffective in the workplace.

What does it mean to be assertive? It means to be open and honest to those around you, even to your boss. To be assertive means to feel free to express new ideas, opinions, and feelings in a professional manner. Bosses appreciate an employee who is respectfully open. **To an employer, the more important aspect of a suggestion is its presentation— not its raw content.**

I am reminded of the dialogue between Andrew Carnegie and one of his employees. The employee approached Carnegie and requested a meeting with him. Mr. Carnegie agreed, and they met. The young man brought a new way of advertising to Mr. Carnegie's attention and assured him that it would save money for the company. Mr. Carnegie disagreed. Still, the young man said, "Okay, you are the boss, but I assure you that I have studied this, and you will lose money."

Mr. Carnegie took to heart what he said and implemented the new idea. That idea saved the company millions of dollars. That young man's name was Charles Schwab. His idea saved the company money; his assertiveness was awarded by promotion.

Charles Schwab brought his suggestion respectfully and confidently. Few employees understand how to do this successfully. If Mr. Schwab had presented the new idea too aggressively, the idea would have been forgotten. If he had timidly shared his idea with Mr. Carnegie and acquiesced at the first sign of disapproval, he would have failed as well.

Be open and honest with those around you, especially your boss. Always present your feelings and opinions in a respectful manner. Don't bring your personal feelings or life into the work environment. If you have an idea, opinion, or feeling, cordially share your thoughts with your employer and coworkers.

You may notice something about the operations of your company that your boss has overlooked. Bringing it to his attention may be very welcomed. Be willing to present new ideas to your boss, but be prepared if he refutes them. Don't take it personally, but accept his decision, knowing that you did what was expected of you.

Assertiveness takes practice, but it can be mastered by anyone. Practice with your spouse, children, friends, and coworkers. Be open and honest yet remain respectful. **Seek to**

understand rather than to be understood. The more you practice, the more assertive you will become.

"Joint Undertakings Stand A Better Chance When They Benefit Both Sides."

- Euripides

LESSON TO LEARN

Derrick used to walk into the office every morning dreading his first encounter of the day with his boss. Mr. O'Neil, the manager of a large accounting firm, was known to be somewhat harsh with his staff. Derrick, a recent graduate from a prestigious school, studied long and hard to make the grades that would qualify him for what he thought would be a career of easy money and cookbook responsibilities.

In school, he devoted hours to studying every financial term and legal loophole, but he nodded off in his human relations and interpersonal communications courses. In his mind, he would be plenty successful as long as he knew everything there was to know about accounting. Mr. O'Neil shattered his hopes. He barked instructions to Derrick from the coldness of his office chair. When Derrick completed them, Mr. O'Neil would utter a gruff, "It's about time," only to be followed by the complaints, "This isn't what I asked for," or "Kid, if you turn in something like this again, it'll be your last assignment in this office."

By the end of each day, Derrick was so frustrated at Mr. O'Neil for his rude manner and caustic remarks that he left in tears. When Derrick finally quit, Mr. O'Neil wondered why such a talented young lad walked away from a dream career without ever mentioning a word of discontent.

11

JOIN THE
TEAM

*"Success Is A Team Sport.
No One Ever Climbs To The Top Alone."*

- Robb Thompson

Selfless teamwork adds value to you, your coworkers, and the future of the company. In any organization, we are bound by a common cause. Until we become inspired by the spirit of teamwork and recognize the role each part plays to lead an organization to success, we forfeit the benefits of teamwork.

What is teamwork? It is a group of individuals that join together to accomplish a single goal. They are agreed in their objective and enthusiastic in their pursuit. Their motive is to add value, not to seek their own good. **A company without trustworthy team players cannot excel.**

Michael Jordan's basketball talent alone couldn't win championships. Only when he developed a teamwork mentality were the championships won. Notice also that the Chicago Bulls won the trophy, not Michael Jordan. No one makes it to the top alone.

True teamwork depends on relating to others in such a way that they cooperate with you. It begins with you. You must first be willing before you can expect others to be. Management expert Peter Drucker says, *"All employees have to see themselves as executives so that they will see the work they do in the context of the entire corporation."*

I constantly remind my employees they are part of a team. They play a role that no one else plays. It is up to them to take care of their responsibilities. Otherwise, the organization doesn't succeed. My personal successes are only possible because of the team that supports me. Not everyone can be the star player. Role players are just as important. Although I may receive most of the credit, I know those who truly deserve it. We are a team, and when the team wins, everyone deserves the credit.

Cultivate the spirit of a team player. Seek to harmonize with your coworkers in the achievement of the organization's vision. Be willing to sacrifice time, credit, money, and effort to enhance the team's potential. A team is only as strong as its weakest player, so make sure to help others grow. Find ways to bring out the best in your teammates. Teamwork costs relatively little for the great dividends it pays.

> *"The Achievements Of An Organization*
> *Are The Results Of The Combined Effort*
> *Of Each Individual."*
>
> *- Vince Lombardi*

LESSON TO LEARN

Interviewing the applicant for the position reminded Mr. Harris of his youthful naiveté. Their conversation started out very cordially as Matt shared some of his past experiences that he thought qualified him for the job. "I always liked wrestling. It was the only sport where I was in complete control of the outcome. I didn't have to depend on anyone to come through for me."

Immediately a red flag went up in Mr. Harris's mind. He knew whoever he hired would need to depend on other members of the company to be successful. He followed through with the rest of the interview, giving Matt a few other questions to answer. The man truly did have some impressive qualifications, but something in his attitude worried Mr. Harris.

Matt left the office that day in high spirits. The next applicant warmly greeted Mr. Harris as he took his seat. A few minutes into the interview, the man mentioned, "I always loved baseball..." Mr. Harris didn't hear the rest of what he said. He chuckled at the irony of the situation. Never before had he realized the common denominator among all of his current employees—the quality that made them effective. Mr. Harris hired this man on the spot, and Matt wondered why he never got a phone call.

RISK DOING SOMETHING
GREAT

12

*"Most People Live And Die With Their Music
Still Unplayed. They Never Dared To Try."*

- Mary Kay Ash

12

I like individuals who are willing to take risks and put themselves on the line to get ahead. They don't fear mistakes or failure. They are unaffected by the opinions of others, which allows them to express themselves freely and openly. When they have an idea, they share it, unafraid of rejection. Their creativity flows because of the freedom in which they live. They willingly invest hours of their personal time on a project, recognizing the possibility that it won't be accepted.

Risk-takers take initiative and make executive decisions. Sometimes such actions get them in trouble, but many times those decisions get them promoted. Going the extra mile in taking risks is worth the effort even if failure is the result, because the experience and growth from the risks are priceless.

- *Are you willing to take risks?*
- *Do you fear to fail or make a mistake?*
- *Do ideas linger within you because you fear you will be rejected?*
- *Do you have a difficult time expressing a new way of doing things because you don't want to be corrected?*

I want risk-takers on my team. Here's how I define a risk-taker: he is someone who collects the facts and knowledge concerning his idea and accurately assesses if the value of its success is worth the price it requires. He has collected enough evidence to support that his risk is good for both the company and for those around him. I do not consider a risk-taker to be the one who makes decisions or presents ideas flippantly. I only want those who are confident that the return is greater than the risk.

STEPS TO DEVELOP RISK-TAKING:

1. **Face the fear of failure.** This one fear aborts many great futures. There are books unwritten, songs unsung, ideas not expressed because of the fear of failure. The only way to conquer the fear of failure is to face it.

2. **Practice taking small risks.** You don't need to start big. Just a little risk here and there gives you confidence to take bigger risks down the road.

3. **Be willing to take responsibility for failure.** Express to those around you that you will take responsibility if something does not succeed. Fortunately, failure is just an opportunity to learn what not to do. But you cannot do this at the expense of the organization. Take risk, but take it responsibly.

4. **Take the risk confidently and enthusiastically.** Many risks fail because people attempt them with too much reserve. Your success calls for a whole-hearted effort. You must take a risk with confidence knowing you will succeed and bring value to the organization.

"Play The Game For More Than You Can Afford
To Lose. Only Then Will You Learn The Game."

- Winston Churchill

Take a moment to read the following poem entitled
<u>The Comfort Zone</u> and see how it relates to you.

THE COMFORT ZONE

I used to have a comfort zone where I knew I wouldn't fail.
The same four walls and busy work were really more like jail.

I longed so much to do the things I'd never done before,
But stayed inside my comfort zone and paced the same old floor.

I said it didn't matter that I wasn't doing much.
I said I didn't care for things like commission checks and such.

I claimed to be so busy with things inside my zone,
But deep inside I longed for something special of my own.

I couldn't let my life go by just watching others win.
I held my breath; I stepped outside and let the change begin.

I took a step and with new strength I'd never felt before,
I kissed my comfort zone goodbye and closed and locked the door.

If you're in a comfort zone, afraid to venture out,
Remember that all winners were at one time filled with doubt.

A step or two and words of praise can make your dreams come true.
Reach for your future with a smile; success is there for you!

LESSON TO LEARN

The British domination of the thirteen colonies began to exasperate the patience of many of the colonists. Among them was a man named Samuel Adams. Adams was a member of the Provincial Assembly, an organization of prominent colonists. When the British soldiers of Boston reacted violently to the citizens' mild disruptions, Adams was appointed to approach the governor to demand the removal of the troops from the city. His request was granted.

Before long, Adams became more and more well known for his opposition of traditional British rule. Fearing rebellion, Governor Gage of Massachusetts offered Adams a worthwhile reward if he would change his position, and punishment if he would not. Here is Adams' reply to the governor's messenger, requesting that Adams make peace with the government:

"Then you may tell Governor Gage that I trust I have long since made my peace with the King of kings. No personal consideration shall induce me to abandon the righteous cause of my country. And, tell Governor Gage it is the advice of Samuel Adams to him, no longer to insult the feelings of an exasperated people."

His response meant no turning back, and it eventually led to the independence of the United States of America. Be willing to take risks and you will experience monumental moments in your own life.

13

MAINTAIN CLEAR FOCUS

"*Your Future Success Is Created By Your Present Focus.*"

- Robb Thompson

13

Focus is vital to your success. In order to reach your final destination, you have to remain focused on your objective. **Once you lock your focus onto a particular goal, refuse to change. Keep your focus until you reach the goal that is set before you.** Proverbs states, "Where there is *no vision*, the people *perish*." People of excellence refuse to break focus because they realize that the consequences of doing so result in great loss.

Those who have failed teach humanity that we must focus on the prize rather than on the price. Broken or misdirected focus mercilessly crushes our hopes. For example, take a young man who attempts to lose weight. His success depends on how firmly he focuses his desire to weigh less and be trim. The moment he focuses on what he does not want, fattening food for example, he begins moving in that direction.

The lesson is that focus only becomes useful when we move toward something we want. It becomes counterproductive when we use it to keep us from something we don't want. **If your focus is on the dreams you have for your life, the world has a way of presenting opportunities to make those dreams a reality.**

Always Move Toward Your Desired Future; Don't Run Away From Your Undesired Past.

I've noticed, after their early thirties, people start reflecting on their lives.

- How did I get here?
- How do I get out of this mess?
- How do I focus on what God called me to?

Many regret the meaninglessness of the life they've lived to that point. Maybe they had dreams at one time, but they lost sight of the day-to-day actions necessary to realize them. They broke their focus, and they failed. I might venture to say that broken focus is the only reason men fail.

Author James Allen said, *"You will become as small as your controlling desire, as great as your dominant aspiration."* Your dominant aspiration is not what you think it is. What you think, it is. In other words, the thoughts you most regularly encourage define your most dominant aspiration.

You may write a lofty dream in a journal, but your true desires are those to which you give the most thought. Your ability to maintain focus causes you to excel in all areas of life, even rising above the unexpected circumstances that come your way. Only focused men and women leave a worthwhile legacy.

Every road traveled has a toll to pay. Temporary setbacks won't debilitate you if you focus on your final destination.

Focus is not a simple task; it is a learned skill that is mastered through much practice. The more you practice, the more precise and passionate you become.

What do you want to accomplish with your life? Having a goal on which to focus supplies the motivation to propel you to the next step. Look for the small completions that give you the momentum to achieve the success you ultimately desire. As you strive for your goals, keep in mind that your aim is not simply to achieve your goal, but to grow as a person. **It is not what you achieve in life that makes it wonderful, but who you become on the journey that determines your true level of achievement.**

The Excellent View Life
Through The Eyes Of Unbroken Focus.

LESSON TO LEARN

Jacob had a good-paying job in the trades. The summers were hard—early mornings and long days in the heat of the sun. Winters, though, balanced his schedule, giving him plenty of time to do whatever he felt like. It wasn't until the third summer that Jacob realized he might be in trouble. Two years had gone by, and he was doing the same thing—heavy labor in mud and sweat. In all that time he had no ambition for something more.

The day-to-day life was tolerable even though he consistently went home sore and muddy. He noticed, though, that both the foreman and the owner left the shop each afternoon in the same clean clothes in which they started the day. From then on, Jacob decided where he'd go in his career. He began picturing himself in the supervisor's position. On the job, he studied the men he wanted to be like and gave up trying to be cool around his buddies.

As expected, Jacob soon was elevated to assistant supervisor. When the next summer came, the surplus of work necessitated another supervisor position, which Jacob was readily awarded.

SET THE STANDARD IN
COMPETENCE

14

"*Competence Is The Non-negotiable Currency On The Road Of Promotion.*"

- Robb Thompson

14

Although employers prefer willingness over competence, the willing still must become competent in a short time for them to remain valuable. Competence does not just know how to do the job—it's the resident expert of the company's department. That is what I look for in an employee. Many times, those who are willing don't receive the promotion because they're not competent or able to handle a higher level of responsibility.

Bosses look for employees that can do what is required flawlessly and repeatedly. Ask yourself:

- *Am I an expert at what I do?*
- *Can I perform difficult tasks efficiently?*
- *Do I require certain skills to enhance my productivity?*
- *What price am I willing to pay for the development of those skills?*

Most of us have heard the story of David, the young shepherd boy, and Goliath, the warrior giant. David defeated Goliath by throwing a stone from a sling; this was a skill that he perfected in his free time. His reward was the king's daughter in marriage and national fame. His next promotion, access to the king's presence, was his reward for his expertise of the harp, another skill he refined in his free time.

You will earn equally great rewards by increasing your competency. One simple way is to use some of your time away from work to develop skills to enhance your everyday performance. As you become more qualified and efficient, you will be credited as an expert, which can only lead to promotion!

> *"The Differences Between A Competent Person And An Incompetent Person Are Demonstrated In His Environment (Surroundings)."*

> *- L. Ron Hubbard*

LESSON TO LEARN

Secretaries don't get as much credit as they deserve. They are some of the hardest working people in any organization. One commercial development company employed an honest, hardworking secretary. With a background in banking and accounting, she was perfect for the job. Before long, though, her tasks became much broader than adding numbers, writing checks, and answering phone calls.

Subcontractors would march into the offices with questions about the development in progress. The company's own employees would approach her with difficulties. Even the owner began to rely on her for vital information. In short, she became so competent with the intricate workings of every aspect of the business that she became irreplaceable.

Her firm but tactful manner of collecting payment, her unsurpassed multitasking ability, and her rain-or-shine reliability made her the hub for every transaction of the company. In addition to her demanding day job, she acquired her CPA from a community college. Her employer rewarded her efforts accordingly.

ESTABLISH AND PRESERVE
ORGANIZATION

15

*"For Every Minute Spent In Organizing,
An Hour Is Earned."*

- Benjamin Franklin

15

Where is that report I finished yesterday? Why can't I find the schedule for the meeting? Paper is everywhere, files are out of place, and I can't even see my desktop!

Is this your life at the office? Clutter in the work area clouds your thinking and inhibits your productivity.

The first step to organization is to clean your work area. Ask for help if necessary. Your productivity depends on it. Though it may take a few hours, it's worth your time. The goal is to structure your area so you work most efficiently. Supplies, tools, and information you use most often should be at your fingertips, readily retrieved and readily replaced.

When you don't have the time to organize, the next best thing is to remove the clutter to a different place while you work. Paper can even be put on the floor if that's what it takes to create a clean desk. You will feel more relaxed and focused.

You will be amazed at the unnecessary things on your desk. We tend to put things on our desk that we don't really need. Instead of putting things where they belong, we throw them on our desk. Go through the things on your desk, and what you don't need, throw away. Why keep unnecessary paperwork?

Business expert, Brian Tracey, has this motto: *When in doubt, I throw it out*. Put your files in an order that's convenient for you. Every file should be clearly labeled in a way you understand so that you can find any document at a moment's notice. Computers also should be accessible in your work area. If you go to another area for computer use, you lose several minutes each time with the distractions of the move.

When your boss visits you in your work area, do you want him to question your competence just because of disorder? You will feel much more confident when he stops by if your area is in order. Even if he does not stop by your work area, you have a better attitude about work when everything is in order. There are so many sources of stress on a job. Why should your personal work space be one?

> *"The Purpose Of Organization Is To Enable Common Men To Do Uncommon Things."*
>
> *-Peter Drucker*

LESSON TO LEARN

As a traveling representative for a cosmetic company, Janet's responsibility was to visit the large department stores in the area. The company let her use a small SUV so she would have enough room for all of her samples and paperwork. The problem, though, wasn't that Janet didn't have enough room for her materials. It was that she never took the time to organize them.

After leaving one department store, she made a quick trip to her vehicle, tossed the order forms on the seat, grabbed what she needed for her next appointment, and arrived with just seconds to freshen up. Her stunning presentation of the company's product made her a sale almost every time, but that didn't make up for her haphazard habit of misplacing important forms. More than once she had to return to a store and request they fill out another order form.

Her seemingly hopeless situation was solved in the most unexpected way. One of the managers to whom she sold her product noticed her disorganization and the problems it created, so she told Janet of her daughter who aspired to work in cosmetics. The young lady was a genius at organization. She was hired at Janet's company and was assigned for training under Janet. Within a week, the new team had both organized their paperwork and increased sales significantly.

RESPECT
NO MATTER WHAT

16

"*What You Respect Travels In Your Direction;*
What You Disrespect Begins Its Exodus
From Your Presence."

-Robb Thompson

16

One of the qualities that brings the greatest return on any investment in the workplace and in other areas of your life is respect. Self-respect is defined as *the due respect for oneself, one's character, and one's conduct; the quality of being worthy of esteem or respect.*

Respecting others becomes possible when we respect ourselves. In fact, our respect for others is in direct proportion to our self-respect. The man who doesn't respect himself cannot possibly show genuine respect for others because it's impossible to give something he doesn't possess. Before you can enhance your respect for others, you first need to address the respect you have for yourself. **Self-respect is the cause and respecting others is the result.**

What is the cause for lack of self-respect? *"There is not a criminal in the world,"* L. Ron Hubbard says, *"whose life of crime cannot be traced to a loss of self-respect."* If we ask a criminal what a loss of self-respect means, we hear the pitiful phrase, "One day I found I couldn't trust myself." Lack of self-respect is directly linked to the confidence one has in their own character.

The stronger your character becomes, the greater your self-respect. The person with self-respect simply likes himself. Self-respect is not contingent on success because there are always failures with which to contend. Neither is it a result of comparing yourself with others, because there is always someone better. Once you cultivate self-respect, you are able to truly respect others.

The law of respect says that you attract what you respect, and you repel what you disrespect. Your promotion is linked to the degree you respect those around and above you. Every relationship grows proportionately to the level of respect you have for it. In marriage, a spouse who is not respected enters self-preservation. Although he or she does not leave the relationship physically, they leave emotionally. On the other hand, marriage partners who show respect to each other are drawn closer through the years.

How can you show respect in the workplace? Here are five simple yet powerful steps to take.

1. **Always address your superior as "Sir" or "Ma'am."** Calling superiors by their first name leads to familiarity, and familiarity breeds contempt. Always address the position, not necessarily the person. An employer is more than willing to listen to any employee who never shows anything but respect.

2. **Don't speak aimlessly.** Before you begin a conversation with your superior, ask if he has a moment to listen. If they know you only speak when addressed and after you have prepared your thoughts, they trust what you say and will give you their time.

3. **Use time on the job for work purposes only.** Respect your boss's time. Don't cut corners or use your time at work for personal phone calls, paying your bills, or socializing with coworkers. You have been given a job. Use your time to get done what has been requested of you.

4. **Practice the Golden Rule.** Treat others as you want them to treat you. Your coworkers are people, too—with the same desires for promotion and increase. See yourself as someone who can help them obtain what they desire. Zig Ziglar said, *"If you help enough other people get what they want, you will certainly get what you want."*

5. **Be willing to do whatever is asked of you.** Show respect to every instruction given to you. Don't do things reluctantly or grudgingly. Do them with a willing attitude. Attitude is possibly the greatest expression of respect. Respecting the assignment shows that you respect the one who requested it of you.

The issue of respect makes a difference in the workplace. Respect guarantees access. Regardless of how your present may be, stay respectful and your situation will turn around.

"Men Are Respectable Only As They Respect."

-Ralph Waldo Emerson

LESSON TO LEARN

One of the best demonstrations of respect in American history is the story of Martin Luther King, Jr. His story has been told every January since 1986 when his birthday was declared a national holiday.

The African-American communities of the southern states were still being treated unjustly almost 100 years after Lincoln signed the Emancipation Proclamation. King, along with many other civil rights leaders, organized non-violent protests against their discriminators. Previous attempts had been made to bring more freedom to the African-Americans, but King's efforts brought lasting success because he chose to respect others. Had he resorted to violence or slander, he would have lived and died without leaving an impact. Instead, his deep respect for himself and his race, coupled with his respect for the human race, created the changes that have so greatly enhanced our society and world today.

COMMUNICATE
EFFECTIVELY

17

"Your Ability To Communicate Is An Important
Tool In Your Pursuit Of Your Goals, Whether
It Is With Your Family And Coworkers
Or Your Clients And Customers."

- Les Brown

There are four aspects of effective communication. Remember, not all communication is verbal. Actions, facial expressions, and posture all communicate a message. Some people unknowingly send the wrong message.

1. **Discretion.** The dictionary defines discretion as *being careful about what one says or does, or the ability to keep silent; regulated by one's own choice.* Discretion is a choice. It is a quality that you develop and master, becoming more discrete as you practice. Keeping quiet is the best way to practice. Talking too much is very destructive. High achievers have learned to guard their conversation carefully, knowing when to speak and when not to speak, what to say and what not to say.

2. **Active Listening.** It is nearly always more profitable to listen than it is to speak. A good listener may hear something that will add to his collection of knowledge. Be attentive to what others say. If you practice active listening by mentally repeating what the other party says a moment after he says it, you will stay alert and grasp the details of the conversation. This takes practice, but soon it will become a part of your everyday conversation.

3. **Clarity.** Be clear with your words. Whenever you attempt to present an idea or the progress of a project, prepare

what you say. Be clear, concise, and candid in every conversation. Allow your boss's questions to carry on the conversation rather than your presentation.

4. **Understanding.** Don't leave the conversation until you understand what is expected of you. Don't feel unprofessional for asking your boss to explain what he wants from you. Write it down. This shows him that you are interested in doing what he says. Gaining a deeper and more clear understanding greatly enhances the final product.

Learning to communicate is crucial in the workplace environment. These are just four main aspects of effective communication. There are many more, but the point is to know with whom you communicate. Everyone needs to be communicated with differently. Always ask yourself: *How will they receive what I am trying to say?* Step into their shoes, then make the decision of whether or not to communicate.

Also, your body language consists of nearly 70% of all communication. How you posture greatly determines how your words are received. This is a skill you must learn if you want to be an excellent employee.

"The Most Important Thing In Communication Is To Hear What Isn't Being Said."

- Peter Drucker

LESSON TO LEARN

A man walked up to the secretary to ask for an apartment application. She tersely replied, "The deadline was yesterday. I can't give you one." The man, perceiving her stubbornness, politely left the office. He proceeded to write her an email, but didn't identify himself as the man in the office until the end of the letter.

He first acknowledged the goal of the company—to make a profit from their tenants. He commented that he understood the necessity to have reliable tenants who abide by policies and pay their rent on time. He then said that he wished to be that kind of tenant, and that the company would benefit greatly from his consistency and respect for the property. He identified himself as the man from the office and requested her graciousness in allowing him to apply, reminding her that it was in the company's best interest.

Upon reading the email, she was so impressed by the man's eloquence and humility that she promptly sent a reply inviting him to pick up an application.

DRESS WELL

"*Good Clothes Open All Doors.*"

-Thomas Fuller

18

A report from Stanford University indicates that your clothes determine 55% of the impression you make on people. Another report claims that the right look can increase your salary by 22%. Seventy-five percent (75%) of U.S. workers admit that personal appearance influences attitudes and professionalism. Good hygiene, good grooming, and clean clothes are never too formal, and ripped clothes, baggy T-shirts, and wrinkled jeans are never appropriate.

If you dress professionally, you feel professional. When in doubt, dress on the formal side because it is always better to err by looking too conventional than underdressed. To an employer, your appearance communicates your judgment and competence.

Proper attire varies from field to field. Banking, accounting, and consulting may call for more conservative business attire. Positions in social services, retail, or technology allow a more relaxed or trendy appearance.

Whether or not we like it, the world forms its first and most lasting impressions of a person by his or her appearance. A well-groomed presentation always attracts attention. People cannot help but notice someone so appealing. An appearance of success attracts favorable attention. People are more willing to embrace a clean-cut, sharp-looking young man than one who is unshaven and unkempt.

Although your clothing doesn't produce success, it effects your self-image. This is a powerful truth. Personally, I dress to make myself feel a certain way. If I dressed according to my feelings, I normally wouldn't wear what I wear. This is one practice that has brought great rewards to my life. I made sure to dress successful even when I wasn't, and soon success became mine!

Make a point to look your best. Don't slack just because you don't feel like taking the time to look good. This practice will greatly enhance your productivity and your self-esteem. Practice this for 30 days and watch the transformation take place right before your eyes.

"Regardless Of How You Feel Inside, Always Try To Look Like A Winner. Even If You Are Behind, A Sustained Look Of Control And Confidence Can Give You A Mental Edge That Results In Victory."

- Arthur Ashe

LESSON TO LEARN

Dale Carnegie tells the story of a young man who began working as a teller at a bank. Rather than dressing like the other tellers, this man observed the wardrobe of the bank manager and dressed similarly. Soon thereafter, the bank's customers, his fellow employees, his superiors, and most importantly, he himself saw him as the bank manager.

Can you guess what happened? Before long, he was promoted to that position, while all the "experienced" tellers remained at their present positions.

CHARACTER
MODEL
19

"Integrity Is The Foundation Upon Which
Your Life's Work Is Built."

- Robb Thompson

19

True success rests on the strength of your character. The success of every great man in history is traced to their sterling public as well as private character. As men of integrity, they accomplished what they set out to do.

Many youths start well and attain moderate success by middle age, but how many people do you know who finish life stronger than their middle years? How many leave a legacy of greatness? Not many, but of those who do, the tie that binds them together is excellent character. They all possess a strong, moral fiber that allows them to build a successful life.

If you desire career success or a name of renown, then you must start by perfecting your character. A skyscraper contractor that overlooks the importance of the foundation and moves on to the building will experience catastrophic failure. The same is true for those who refuse to invest many years refining their character.

Others may surpass you momentarily, but if you choose character first, you make your mark in the end. I would rather achieve promotion gradually through ethical means than to achieve it quickly, cutting corners and cheating and betraying others. Character is lacking among employees in America. People cheat on their timecards, steal time during the day, use their work time for personal benefit, talk bad about their employer or other coworkers, the list goes on and on. You have experienced people like this. It is a sad truth, but in today's age, these practices are acceptable.

Don't allow yourself the luxury of compromising. Stay true to your character, do what is asked of you, and respect the time and position of the one who asked you for it. It will pay off in the end. Be patient and you will see the importance of strong moral character.

It Is Impossible For Your Life To Produce Anything Beyond The Strength Of Your Moral Fiber.

LESSON TO LEARN

As a recent newlywed and soon to be daddy, William quickly found out that his job in retail wasn't going to pay the bills. He decided to take a job as a salesman for a local car dealership. Though he had little experience with cars, he was a candid communicator and an avid learner. Over the years, he built a reputation as an honest man, and many customers returned to him for subsequent purchases.

Twenty-five years later, William's older son had graduated college and moved out of state, and his younger was in his third year of service in the U.S. Army. William and his wife were ready to escape the hustle of city life. A life in the suburbs looked very appealing. Having said goodbye to his coworkers and customers, he and his wife moved to small town a few hours from the city. Of course, William still needed to work, so once again applied at a local dealership.

The transition was quite smooth, but before long, William was told to "forget" some details when customers were interested in purchasing a used car—details that would likely change a customer's mind. William refused to do so. He had built a career on character, and he wasn't about to demolish his foundational values. Yes, his commission wasn't as impressive as it could have been, but his reputation was sterling. And that helped him to sleep at night—something money could never do for him.

COMMIT
TO CONSTANT CHANGE

20

"Pay The Price Of Change To Obtain The
Prize Of Achievement."

- Robb Thompson

Wouldn't it be wonderful if our success would just come to us? Wouldn't it be great if we could wake up each day, knowing that our lives were going to work themselves out, and that we were going to become all we need to become just because we got up? I would love that! But unfortunately, that is not the case. All success in life is a result of positive change.

For some, changes happen by accident. These changes are often a result of a person refusing to make a decision and then being forced into a situation that they otherwise would have avoided. Painful consequences are right around the corner, so they jam on the brakes, make a dangerous U-turn, and just barely avoid disaster. That kind of change can never lead to any real success. All it does is keep a life from completely self-destructing.

Have you ever seen this happen, either to you or to a coworker? Maybe you saw it when it pretty much became mandatory for every person to know how to operate a personal computer. Some people likely saw what was coming and prepared for it; others reluctantly changed because they saw their job security threatened. Changes like these are like walking the plank with a pinkslip-sword to your back: either you give in to the demands of the market and the workplace or you fall to the crashing low-level positions below. To make things worse, there's usually a cruise ship sailing by, and all the people who changed ahead of time are dancing by the poolside!

You don't have to find yourself in such a situation. You can get on the cruise ship of promotion, job security, and career fulfillment, but the boarding platform is called, **"CHANGE."** There, you need to sign an agreement to abide by the rules of the ship—excellence, faithfulness, respect, etc. All of your luggage has to pass through a mediocrity detector. If the detector sounds, you'll be asked to leave. Once you're aboard, you have to leave behind your land-locked ways of thinking—old skills, old best-practices, and old achievements are only added weight on this cruise ship. All of it has to be jettisoned. The ocean, unlike land, is always flowing; nothing stays the same. The ship and all its passengers have to be ready to flow with it.

Physics teaches that the natural course for everything is to move towards disorder. Without continuous applied effort, our world starts to fall apart. At home, the house gets messy. The laundry piles up. The car rusts. The lawn gets overgrown. The bills keep coming. The children need new clothes.

The workplace is no exception. Coworkers grow cold and familiar. Bosses lose the respect they once had. Clients become a lesser priority. Showing up late becomes acceptable. Conversation declines into gossip and complaints. Nothing changes for the better all on its own.

Fortunately, virtually anything can change for the better with continuous applied effort. Back to physics, the universe as a whole moves toward disorder, but any one system can become ever more organized and sophisticated when the right forces are channeled toward a goal. On the job, coworkers can become warmer and more considerate. Employees can uphold their boss's honor. Clients can remain top priority. Standard policies can be observed. Conversation can grow more pleasant and truthful. They simply must put in the effort to do so. Left alone, thoughts and attitudes go downhill. Guarded, thoughts and attitudes climb higher and higher.

Have you made the choice to be a person given to positive change? At this point, people often shout the question, *"What do I change!?"* The answer they hear back is, *"You!"* The first step is to become a person of change. When you do, you see all the things around you that need a touch-up (or an overhaul). You have no trouble finding areas and practices to implement changes. Once you change, every necessary change will jump out at you.

Any promotion or progress made in the workplace that violates the laws of ethical character eventually leads to loss. A person who denies the role character plays in success has a very poor understanding of the way the universe works. Since character is such a vital part of success in the workplace, a discussion of change wouldn't be complete without it. This truth, that positive change is a result of choice, affects our character and our way of thinking as much as it does our world at home and at the workplace. None of these will improve without direct, conscious effort. True, positive change is always a result of personal choice.

Have you made the choice to be a person of character? Have you seen your life as it could be, or have you resigned to the natural course of things? You have within yourself the ability to become whoever and whatever you desire. How far you go is determined only by the price you are willing to pay.

Each of us has a certain degree of insight into our own flaws and shortcomings; we can and must change them by ourselves. But each of us also has blind spots that are detrimental to our future success if we don't address them. For these, we need the help of those closest to us.

Here is a challenge: **make a practice of asking your closest friends and family members what they would change about you.** Ask your boss and trustworthy coworkers the same thing. You may be surprised or even upset by their answers, but therein lies the key to success. Change. As you open yourself to the suggestions of these people, you'll start taking steps closer to becoming the person you must be—at home, on the job, and in your character.

> *Genuine Fulfillment And Personal Satisfaction*
> *Are The Result Of Constant Change.*

LESSON TO LEARN

Having worked his way up the company for nearly seven years, Mark wasn't too thrilled when he heard that the majority of his department was being outsourced. Only the top-tiers of management would retain their positions. The rest of the staff would be shuffled around the company or be released. The years Mark spent in technical and management training weren't going to do him much good now. He'd have to start again in what would be akin to an entry-level position, though the company found creative ways to avoid such terminology. Mark wasn't as frustrated with the slight pay cut as he was with the feeling of wasted years.

Starting over was not something he had planned on. Nevertheless, he did remember the mass email he received a year earlier from the department head that encouraged the staff to learn a foreign language. The company was even willing to pay for language-learning software for the employees that were interested. Mark, along with most of his coworkers, deleted the email before he even finished reading it. In retrospect, that email may have been his opportunity, not just for job security, but for significant promotion. Oh well. Maybe there will be another opportunity. Maybe. Maybe not.

THE NEXT STEP

Although not exhaustive, the everyday character traits outlined in this book are practical, proven, and time tested. These qualities work together to make up what we know as a successful employee. If you are diligent to put what you learned in this book into practice, you quickly will become successful wherever you work. I do not imply that you will get a raise in 90 days or earn the promotion you've always desired, but you will feel satisfied and your improvement won't go unnoticed.

Use this as a handbook for everyday ways to enjoy success at work. Take it with you when you go to work. Take one quality, read over it, and practice it until it becomes natural to you. You may already possess many of these qualities. But often it is not what we do that makes the difference, it is what we don't do that matters.

Take what you learn and share it with co-workers and challenge them to grow as employees. Always remember, your value to your employer is not what you say you can do, but what you do.

I wish you well as you travel through the terrain of success at work!

LEADERS UNITED

EXCELLENCE IN BUSINESS INTERNATIONAL is a new, exciting, and unique business association created with you in mind! This association was formed to unite business leaders, including entrepreneurs and corporate executives, in a dynamic network providing information, education, and support. Our desire is for you to experience success, not just in business, but in every area of your life! We are committed to assist you in succeeding financially, relationally, in your community, and in your home.

FULFILLING THE PURPOSE FOR YOUR LIFE becomes possible only when you embrace the right relationships. More than any other ingredient, your relationships determine the outcome of your life. With the right people in your life, there is NO LIMIT to what you are able to accomplish, both personally and professionally.

Because we understand how important networks are to you, we invite you to join Excellence in Business International. Through EBI, you will establish networks with people who are PASSIONATE ABOUT SUCCESS and dedicated to excellence.

In addition to connecting you with like-minded businessmen and businesswomen, joining EBI also makes available to you these benefits:

- Networking opportunities, locally and globally

- Inspirational and informative monthly gatherings

- Business and leadership conferences featuring renowned speakers

- Personal Executive Coaching

- Business Consulting Services

- Management and Employee Training

- Corporate Chaplaincy Services

- Extensive Business and Leadership Resource Library

EXCELLENCE IN BUSINESS INTERNATIONAL

DISCOVER
YOUR TRUE POTENTIAL

Everyone needs a coach in life—someone to encourage you, hold you accountable, challenge you, and thrust you beyond your potential curve! Unlike counseling, coaching unlocks your true potential. Personalized coaching has been proven to be the most effective way to cultivate personal and professional skills.

Dr. Robb Thompson is serious about results. After nearly 30 years of learning, mentoring, and teaching simple but life change principles, Dr. Thompson has developed a system of personal transformation that will work for anyone who desires to change.

FOR MORE INFORMATION, CALL OR EMAIL!

708.614.9896
coach@robbthompson.com

ROBB THOMPSON
COACHING